Pace Your Self

A 30-Day Journey to Finding Your Rhythm

Jon A. Parker, PhD

Baleka Wellness Publishing
www.balekawellness.com

Published by Baleka Wellness Publishing
Gainesville, Florida

ISBN: 979-8-9942335-0-4

Cover design by Jon A. Parker
Interior design by Jon A. Parker
Printed in the United States of America

This book is intended for educational and informational purposes only and is not a substitute for professional medical or mental health advice. If you are in need of support, please consult a qualified mental health professional.

Preface

I want to start this journey by telling you about the moment I realized I had built a thriving, beautiful life on an utterly unsustainable foundation.

For years, my professional identity was defined by seeking fulfillment through intense effort. Before becoming a Licensed Professional Counselor, I navigated careers as a licensed tax preparer, a personal banker, a tour guide, a journalist, and even a Grammy-nominated audio engineer. Each role was a pursuit of my "true calling," yet I was always left with the same struggle many men face: finding meaning in life and fulfillment through work and play.

Like many men, I believed strength meant pushing harder while never stopping or showing weakness. This approach served me well enough to earn multiple degrees, including a Master of Arts in Marriage and Family Therapy and a PhD in Youth Development and Family Sciences. My academic journey at the University of California, Berkeley, instilled in me the values of justice, equality, and speaking up for the voiceless, which drove me toward community service and clinical practice; however, I found myself moving away from chill to chaos, always pushing and always chasing while never feeling fulfilled.

The pivotal moment that forced me to reconcile my professional expertise with my personal pace did not happen in a counseling room or a research lab; it happened on the southern tip of Africa, on a public road, in intense pain.

The Genesis of a Mantra

The phrase "Pace Your Self" was born from a painful personal failure in 2019 at the Two Oceans Marathon in Cape Town. I had spent months training, reminding myself to set a sustainable pace once the starter pistol fired. As founder of Baleka Run Club (BRC), I knew the importance of pace. Initially, BRC started as a training space for this race, but it evolved into something much broader. As people gathered to prepare physically for the marathon, the conversations that unfolded during group walks, trail runs, and hikes revealed shared struggles related to stress, purpose, relationships, and balance. Movement became the entry point, but wellness became the mission.

Out of this experience, Baleka Wellness was formed as a community that emphasized participation, connection, and sustainability. The focus shifted from performance and comparison to showing up consistently, listening to the body, and supporting one another. So, the lessons learned between BRC and Baleka Wellness had me well prepared for the marathon.

But, when the race began, all rational training vanished, and I succumbed to a universal male impulse to keep up with the crowd: to run another man's race.

My competitive drive aggravated an existing Iliotibial Band (IT Band) injury, and because I didn't keep MY pace, by stopping or slowing down to a manageable jog, I had to limp for more than two hours to finish the race. My gun time was 03:01:37. The failure to pace myself almost cost me the medal and undid months of training.

In that excruciating, final mile, the mantra of this book crystallized: running another man's race is detrimental to long-term success and well-being. The core lesson was that I needed to check in with *my* gauges and respect *my* limits. I needed to pace my self.

In the book's mantra, Your Self is intentionally separated because it emphasizes that you are uniquely created to run your own race, and you must set your own pace. I realized the pain points of burnout, comparison, and failure to honor my body's limits that I experienced during the marathon in Cape Town is the epidemic affecting men today.

When the Pace Becomes the Problem: Helping Men Find a Sustainable Rhythm

Today, too many men are struggling with life transitions, self-esteem challenges, relationship difficulties, and stress management. Most men wait for a crisis to admit their struggles; they push until something breaks, whether it's their health, relationships, or peace of mind. In my private practice, I have worked with professional athletes, entertainers, and business professionals who, despite outward success, experience burnout, emotional fatigue, and difficulty honoring their internal limits.

This book is the antidote to that frantic sprint.

Pace Your Self is the synthesis of my painful lesson in South Africa and the clinical work I have undertaken with men who are struggling to sustain the pace of modern life. I intentionally integrate nature-based methodology into my clinical framework because movement or relaxation through restorative environments has a powerful ability to reduce stress, regulate the nervous system, and create space for reflection. This approach began in Cape Town, South Africa, through Baleka Wellness and was reinforced through my doctoral research that examined how nature-based interventions support mental health and sustainable well-being.

The practices in this book are not based on opinion or trends. They are grounded in decades of research showing how movement and nature restore attention, reduce stress, and support nervous system regulation. In this framework, nature is not simply a backdrop for healing, but an active and essential component of growth. For readers interested in the scientific foundation of this approach, a summary of the research is provided in the Appendix.

Together, the evolution of Baleka Wellness, the formation of the Baleka Run Club, my clinical work, and my research shaped the foundation of *Pace Your Self*. The 30-day curriculum in this book offers an accessible pathway for men to slow down, reconnect with themselves, and build a rhythm that supports long-term resilience. In this practical roadmap, the clinical insights, nature-based practices, and lived experiences described above are organized into a clear structure designed to help you slow down without losing momentum.

The Pace Your Self Roadmap

This 30-day plan replaces the unsustainable "grind" with a structured, resilient rhythm. It is divided into four critical weeks: Week 1 helps you *Wake Up to Your Pace*; Week 2 integrates *Move Your Body, Clear Your Head*; Week 3 *Return to Nature* reconnects you to nature; and Week 4 *Become the Man You're Meant to Be* supports you in solidifying the man you are becoming.

Each day follows a simple, repeatable rhythm designed to meet you where you are. You'll be invited to pause, notice, move, and reflect in small, practical ways that fit real life. Each day ends with a Daily Anchor. These are not affirmations meant to hype you up or override your reality. They are anchors, short statements designed to help you notice, choose, and return to a sustainable rhythm.

This book is not about perfection; it is about providing a daily check-in where you can be honest, reset, and take one small step. You don't need heroic effort. You need patience, self-compassion, and small consistent steps.

The truth is your life is not a sprint; it's a long, personal race with your name on it. I learned that lesson the painful way, by pushing past my limits, ignoring the signals, and paying for it mile after mile. You don't have to learn that way. This book is designed to help you recognize the warning signs early, slow down before damage is done, and build a rhythm that keeps you strong instead of broken. Let me show you how to find your unique pace so you can keep running your race, steady and strong, through every inch, every foot, and every mile of your life.

Introduction

Become the Man You Need Now

Modern life rewards speed, endurance, and constant output. Many men are taught, explicitly or implicitly, that success comes from pushing harder, staying busy, and ignoring internal warning signs. Over time, that mindset can lead to exhaustion, disconnection, and a sense that life is moving faster than you can sustain.

When men operate in a constant state of urgency, the nervous system never fully recovers. Chronic stress affects sleep, mood, concentration, physical health, and relationships. Over time, the body adapts to pressure by staying "on," making it harder to rest, think clearly, or feel connected. Many men don't notice this shift until something breaks.

Pace Your Self offers a different approach

Pacing is not about doing less; it is about doing what matters in a way that your mind and body can sustain. Learning to pace yourself allows you to stay engaged in your work, your relationships, and your purpose without burning out in the process.

This book is built on one simple but powerful idea: long-term strength is not created by intensity alone, but by rhythm. Sustainable growth happens when you learn to listen to your body, regulate your nervous system, and move through life at a pace that allows you to remain grounded, present, and resilient. Rather than asking you to overhaul your life or adopt extreme habits, this book invites you to develop awareness, consistency, and self-trust...one day at a time.

Why Movement and Nature Are Essential

For many men, especially those who work indoors, rely heavily on technology, or avoid the outdoors, movement and nature can feel optional, inconvenient, or uncomfortable. This book treats them differently: as foundational tools for mental clarity and emotional regulation.

Research consistently shows that regular movement and exposure to natural environments help lower stress, improve focus, and support emotional balance (see Appendix). Even brief periods of walking, stretching, or time near natural light can calm the nervous system and restore mental energy. These benefits are not limited to hikers, runners, or "outdoor people." They apply to men across lifestyles, professions, and personalities.

That's why this book emphasizes flexibility. If going outside feels like a stretch, alternatives are provided, such as grounding exercises near a window or brief, intentional movement indoors. The goal is not perfection or performance, but participation. Small, consistent actions have measurable effects over time.

How to Approach This Book

This book works best when approached with curiosity rather than urgency. You are encouraged to move through it at your own pace, engage honestly with the reflections, and experiment with the practices even when they push you slightly outside your comfort zone. Growth often happens through consistent, manageable steps rather than dramatic change.

You do not need to become someone else to benefit from this process. You simply need to show up as you are.

Life is not a race to be won by keeping up with others. It is a personal journey that requires awareness, patience, and care. The pages that follow are an invitation to slow down, check in, and begin moving forward in a way that allows you to stay steady, grounded, and whole.

1 Raise Your Hand

"Change starts the moment you quietly admit, 'I'm not okay with staying the same.'"

Most men wait for a crisis to raise their hand. They grind, numb out, and tell themselves they'll "figure it out later" until something breaks: health, relationship, career, or peace of mind. If you're holding this book, there's already a part of you that knows your current pace isn't sustainable. Maybe you're exhausted but can't slow down or bored but can't get moving. Either way, today is not about fixing everything. Today is about something much simpler and braver: admitting to yourself that something has to shift.

Your pace is yours. "Pace Your Self" isn't about turning you into a different man; it's about helping you stop running a race that doesn't fit you. For the next 30 days, this book will be your daily check-in, a quiet space where you can be honest, reset, and take one small step. You don't have to tell anyone else you're doing this. But, you do need to tell yourself the truth: you want better, and you're willing to show up.

Today's Nudge:
Pick a specific time of day you'll read each entry (morning coffee, lunch break, before bed) and commit to it. That's your "Pace Moment."

Daily Anchor: "Today, I raise my hand and admit I'm ready for something better."

Reflection

- What made you pick up this book now, not six months ago?
- What are you afraid might happen if nothing changes?

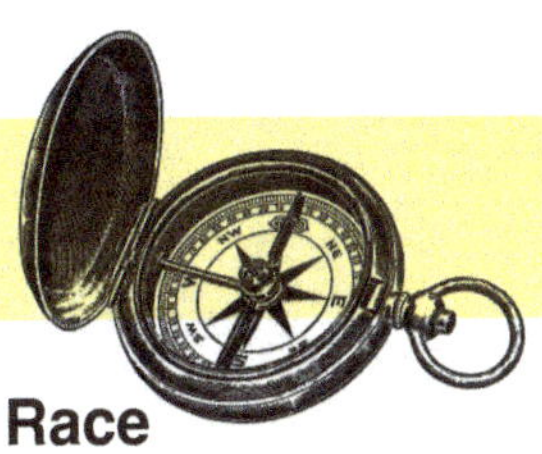

2 Your Pace, Your Race

"You are not behind; you are on your path."

It's easy to feel like you're losing. Social media and casual conversations make it sound like everyone else your age is more successful, more fit, more confident, more "together." That constant comparison quietly kills your motivation because your progress never feels good enough. The truth is you're not running their race. You're running yours: with your history, your wiring, your responsibilities, and your scars. Comparing paces is like comparing shoes; what works for them will blister you.

Today, instead of measuring yourself against other men, measure yourself against your yesterday. Did you show up a little more than you did last week? Did you choose one slightly healthier option, one more honest thought, one moment of courage? That's pace. That's progress. When you stop sprinting to keep up and start walking at your pace, you suddenly have energy to go farther than you thought.

Today's Nudge:

Notice one area where you've been judging yourself as "behind." Reframe it as "on my path," even if it's not where you want to stay. For example, instead of "I'm behind because I'm 35 and don't own a home," try: "I am on my path of building financial stability at a pace that respects my responsibilities." If you tend to be more reflective, you might write: "I am on my path of learning to prioritize peace, and if owning a home is part of that path, I'll make that choice with joy, not pressure."

Daily Anchor: *"I will stop racing other men and start owning my pace."*

Reflection

- Who do you most compare yourself to and how does that affect your pace?
- What changes when you imagine only comparing yourself to yesterday's you?

3 Feel Your Feet

"When your mind is racing, your body can bring you back home."

Most of the time, stress lives in your head as noise: overthinking, replaying conversations, worrying about the future. But your body has been quietly carrying that stress: tight jaw, shallow breathing, clenched shoulders, restless legs, teeth grinding at night. You can't think your way out of being overwhelmed. You have to feel your way back into your body. One of the simplest ways to do that is to literally feel your feet on solid ground.

Today, step outside if you can. Stand still for a moment. Notice how the ground holds your weight without effort. Feel your heels, toes, and the way your body naturally adjusts to balance. You don't have to "empty your mind" or be good at meditation. Just notice: the air on your skin, the sounds around you, and your breath going in and out. This practice is you stepping out of the mental spin and into the present moment. It's not complicated, but it is powerful.

Today's Nudge:
Spend 3-5 minutes standing outside (don't be afraid to go barefoot) or near an open window, focusing only on the sensation of your feet and your breath. Leave the phone behind.

Daily Anchor: "When my mind races, I return to my breath and my feet."

Reflection

- Where in your body do you tend to store stress?
- What did you notice when you slowed down long enough to feel your feet?

4 Check Your Gauges

"A well-paced life is built on honest daily check-ins, not guess-work."

If your car's dashboard lights were broken, you'd constantly risk running out of gas or overheating the engine. Most men live that way with their bodies and minds: no gauges, no regular checks, just pushing until something fails. You don't have to turn yourself into a biohacker to do better. You just need a simple, honest way to notice how you're doing instead of running on autopilot every day.

Think of four basic gauges: sleep, energy, mood, and tension. Each morning and night, you can quickly rate them from 1-10 in your head or on paper. You're not judging yourself; you're collecting data on your life. When you see patterns, such as always tired, always tight, or always irritated, you can make changes from awareness instead of denial. That's how you begin to pace yourself on purpose, not by accident.

Today's Nudge:
This morning and tonight, quickly rate your sleep, energy, mood, and tension from 1-10. Just notice, no fixing yet.

Daily Anchor: "I respect myself enough to check my gauges."

Reflection

- Which "gauge" surprised you when you actually paid attention?
- If one of them is consistently low, what might that be trying to tell you?

5 Slow the Scroll

"Not everything that demands your attention deserves your attention."

Phones aren't evil, but they are designed to hijack your pace. Endless scrolling quietly eats the time and mental space you say you don't have for movement, exercise, reflection, or being outside. You go in "for a minute" and come out 30 minutes later, more restless and less grounded. The problem isn't just the content; it's the constant stimulation that keeps your brain buzzing and your body parked.

Slowing the scroll isn't about becoming a monk. It's about taking back a small piece of your attention and giving it to your real life. When you put your phone down and step outside, even for a few minutes, you give your nervous system a break from flashing lights, noise, and comparison. You remind yourself that the world is bigger than a screen and that your life is happening right now, not just in notifications.

Today's Nudge:
Choose one block of time today (15-30 minutes) where you intentionally stay off your phone and, if possible, spend at least part of it outside.

Daily Anchor: "My attention is valuable, and I choose where it goes."

Reflection

- When are you most likely to scroll without thinking?
- What did you feel during your no-phone block: bored, anxious, peaceful?

6 Breathe Like You Mean It

"Your breath is the simplest reset button you keep forgetting you have."

When you're stressed, your breath usually gets shallow and fast, but you rarely notice it. This type of shallow, fast breathing keeps your body in a low-level fight-or-flight mode, even when you're just checking email or sitting in traffic. Breathing deeper and slower is not some mystical practice reserved for yogis; it's one of the most practical tools you have to calm your system. You carry it everywhere, and it costs nothing.

Today, you're not trying to become a breathwork expert. You're just going to take a few minutes to breathe on purpose. If you can, step outside or stand by an open window. Breathe in through your nose, feeling your ribs expand, and breathe out through your mouth a little longer than you breathed in. Repeat this type of breathing for a few minutes and notice how it feels. You may still have problems to solve afterward, but you'll be facing them with a slightly calmer body and clearer head.

Today's Nudge:
Take one 3-minute break today to breathe slowly and intentionally, preferably outside or by a window. Count your inhales and slightly longer exhales.

Daily Anchor: "I can slow my pace any time by slowing my breath."

Reflection

- How did your body feel before and after those 3 minutes?
- What makes it hard to stop and breathe on purpose during your day?

7 Week One Debrief

"Progress starts when you pay attention to what's happening, not what you wish was happening."

You just made it through Week 1. Maybe you did every nudge, maybe only a few. Either way, this isn't a pass/fail test; it's information. The goal of this week was simple: to wake you up to your pace: to how you're moving, thinking, breathing, and reacting. Most men burnout or drift off course because they never pause long enough to look at the pattern. You're doing that right now.

Take a moment to look back over the last six days. When did you feel most grounded or clear? Was it during a moment of stillness, standing outside, breathing, or simply being honest with yourself? When did you feel most scattered or drained? These clues matter. They show you what supports your best pace and what constantly drags you away from it. Going forward, your job isn't to be perfect. It's to notice, adjust, and keep showing up.

Today's Nudge:
Spend a few minutes reviewing Days 1-6. Write down three things you did from this week's nudges and one small change you already notice in your mood, body, or thinking.

Daily Anchor: "I'm paying attention to my life, and that alone is changing my pace."

Reflection

- What worked best for you this week?
- What almost knocked you off your pace?
- How do you want Week 2 to feel different?

8 Set Your Baseline

"The right minimum is better than the perfect plan."

Most guys swing between two extremes: "go hard or go home" or "I'll start next week." Big fitness plans feel exciting for about three days, then life hits and the whole thing collapses. What actually changes a man's life isn't a heroic workout streak; it's a small, steady movement baseline that he does even on rough days. Your baseline is the "no matter what" version of movement that fits your real life, not your fantasy life.

This week, you're not trying to become an athlete; you're just choosing a floor you won't drop below. It might be a 5-minute walk, 10 squats, or one lap around the block. It should almost feel "too easy" that's the point. When it's simple enough to do even on low-motivation days, you give yourself a real shot at consistency. From there, you can always do more. But, your baseline protects your pace when you don't feel like it.

Today's Nudge:
Choose a daily movement baseline you can realistically do every day this week (for example, a 5-minute walk). Commit to it in writing.

Daily Anchor: "I choose a movement baseline that I can keep, not a plan I'll abandon."

Reflection

- In the past, how have "all-or-nothing" workout plans burned you out?
- What feels like an honest, sustainable baseline for the man you are right now?

9 Walk It Out

"A short walk can shift what a long overthinking session never will."

You don't always need another podcast, book, or deep talk to clear your head. Sometimes, you just need to put one foot in front of the other and let your brain catch up to your body. Walking is one of the most underrated tools you have. It gets your blood moving, loosens up tight muscles, and gives your thoughts room to breathe. Outside, each step reminds you that life exists beyond your screen and your worries.

Today, treat your walk like a moving reset, not a race. If you can, leave your headphones off for at least part of it. Look up. Notice your surroundings: the sky, the trees, the buildings, the sounds. Let your mind wander. You might notice that problems feel less stuck when your body is in motion. Even if nothing "big" changes, you'll likely return with a slightly lighter mood and a clearer head. That's not nothing. That's how you nudge your pace in a better direction.

Today's Nudge:
Take at least one intentional walk today, even if it's just around the block. Spend a few minutes of it without any audio, just noticing what's around you.

Daily Anchor: "When my mind feels heavy, I let my feet help me carry the weight."

Reflection

- How did you feel going into your walk vs. coming out of it?
- What kinds of thoughts showed up once your body started moving?

10 Strong, Not Perfect

"Your body doesn't need perfection; it needs partnership."

A lot of men avoid working out because they feel if they can't do it "right" or "hard enough," it doesn't count. That mindset keeps you stuck on the couch. The truth is your body doesn't care if your push-ups aren't perfect or your squats aren't textbook. It cares that you show up. Strength isn't just muscle; it's the relationship you build with your body over time.

Today, instead of chasing the perfect routine, give your body a small sign of respect. Do a simple bodyweight sequence at your level: push-ups against a wall or counter if you need to or on the floor if you can. Do squats holding onto a chair or deeper if your knees allow. The goal is not to impress anyone. The goal is to remind your body, "I haven't forgotten you. We're in this together." That message, repeated over time, changes how you carry yourself.

Today's Nudge:
Do one short bodyweight session today (push-ups, squats, or similar) at a level that feels challenging but doable. Keep it simple.

Daily Anchor: "I'm not chasing perfection; I'm building a stronger partnership with my body."

Reflection

- What stories do you tell yourself about why you "can't" work out?
- How does it feel to give your body even a small, imperfect dose of strength work?

11 Your Body Isn't the Enemy

"The way you talk to your body shapes the way you live in it."

Many men speak to their bodies like they're disappointments or problems to fix: too soft, too small, too broken, too tired. That constant criticism makes it harder to care for yourself because you're trying to take care of something you secretly resent. Your body has been with you through every season, every late night, and every stress storm. It has absorbed hits and kept you moving, even when you didn't treat it well.

Today is not about pretending everything is perfect. It's about shifting from an adversarial relationship with your body to a respectful one. Notice what your body does for you: how it lets you carry groceries, hug people, climb stairs, laugh, and show up. When you see it less as an enemy and more as a teammate, movement becomes less punishment and more partnership. That shift makes consistent care possible.

Today's Nudge:
Write down at least three things you genuinely appreciate about your body. You'll get no prompts or examples on this. Take your time, think deeply, and appreciate yourself.

Daily Anchor: "My body is my teammate, not my enemy."

Reflection

- How have you been speaking to your body lately?
- If your body could answer you back, what might it say?

12   Sweat Out the Static

"Sometimes, the fastest way to clear your head is to raise your heart rate."

Mental noise builds up like static as unfinished tasks, worries, or tension from the day. Talking about it has value, but sometimes, your nervous system needs a physical outlet more than another analysis session. Pushing yourself just a little physically within your limits can shake loose some of that static. You don't have to crush yourself; you just have to move enough to feel a difference.

Today, pick a form of movement that gets your heart rate up even slightly. It could be brisk walking, climbing stairs, a short jog, a bike ride, a quick set of bodyweight circuits, or even intense yard work. The point is to feel your body working. Notice your breathing, your muscles, and the sweat. When you're done, pay attention to how your mind feels. Problems may still exist, but you might feel less trapped inside them.

Today's Nudge:
Do one activity today that makes you breathe harder than usual for at least a few minutes. Choose something that fits your current fitness level.

Daily Anchor: "I use my body to help clear my mind."

Reflection

- What did you notice about your mood and thoughts after you broke a light sweat?
- How does your body feel when you give it a chance to work?

13 Rest Is Part of the Program

"Rest is not quitting; it's what allows you to keep going."

Many men treat rest like a reward they have to earn or a sign of weakness. So, they push until they crash, then they feel guilty for stepping back. But every good training plan, physical or mental, includes recovery. Muscles grow stronger when they rest between efforts, not when they're constantly strained. Your mind works the same way. If you never pause, your pace becomes frantic instead of sustainable.

Today, think of rest as a strategic investment, not a luxury. You're not "doing nothing;" you're rebuilding the system that carries you through your days. Even a short, intentional rest, such as lying down for 10 minutes, sitting quietly outside, or going to bed a bit earlier, can reset your energy. The key is to rest on purpose, not just collapse when you're wiped out. That's what separates pacing yourself from running yourself into the ground.

Today's Nudge:
Schedule one short, intentional rest block today (10-20 minutes) and actually honor it: no phone and no multitasking. Just breathe and let your body reset.

Daily Anchor: "Rest is part of my strength, not proof of my weakness."

Reflection

- What beliefs do you hold about rest and "being a man?"
- How might those beliefs be affecting your health and your pace?

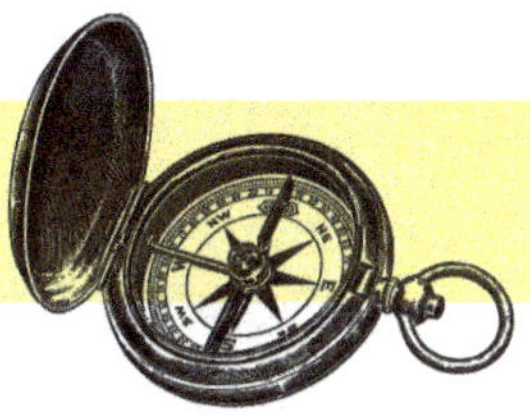

14 Week Two Debrief

"Your body keeps score of how you treat it, and it's starting to notice the difference."

You've just spent a week paying more attention to movement, strength, breath, and rest. Maybe you nailed your baseline every day. Maybe you missed some or most. Either way, this journey isn't about perfection. It's about data and honesty. What did your body tell you this week? Did you sleep any better? Did you notice any small changes in mood, focus, or confidence on days you moved your body?

This is where "Pace Your Self" becomes real. You're beginning to see how your physical pace directly affects your mental and emotional pace. If you felt better on the days you moved, even just a little, that's proof that your body responds to care. If you struggled to do anything, that's useful information too. It shows you where resistance shows up, so you can plan around it instead of pretending it's not there. Next week, you'll begin widening the lens, by letting the environment around you help set the pace you're learning to feel inside.

Today's Nudge:
Look back on Days 8-13. Write down what your baseline ended up being and one change (big or small) you noticed in your body or mood.

Daily Anchor: "I'm learning how my body and mind work together, and I adjust my pace with that wisdom."

Reflection

- What helped you move more this week?
- What got in the way?
- How do you want your relationship with movement to look one month from now?

15 Choose Your Ground

"Where you stand shapes how you feel."

You've been moving more and paying attention to your body. Now, it's time to choose a physical environment that supports the man you're becoming. Nature isn't just scenery; it affects your nervous system. A quiet sidewalk with trees, a local park, a bench by a pond, or even a small courtyard can become your landing pad, a spot where your brain starts to associate "here" with "slow down, breathe, reset." When you pick a default outdoor spot, you make it easier to step out of noise and into clarity.

You don't need the perfect view. You just need a place that's reasonably safe, accessible, and calm enough for you to be there alone with your thoughts. By returning to the same ground regularly, you create a subtle ritual: "When my feet touch this place, my pace changes." Over time, just thinking about that spot can help you reset when life feels loud.

Today's Nudge:
Pick one outdoor spot you can realistically visit several times a week. Go there today, even briefly, and mentally claim it as your "Pace Your Self" ground.

Daily Anchor: "I choose ground that supports the pace I want to live at."

Reflection

- What drew you to this spot?
- How does your body feel when you stand or sit there compared to being indoors or on your phone?

16 Stand Like a Tree

"Strength is being rooted and flexible at the same time."

A healthy tree doesn't rush. It doesn't try to be the tree next to it. It grows at its pace, rooted deeply enough to stand through storms and flexible enough to bend with the wind. Many men try to live like steel poles instead - rigid, unbending, pretending nothing affects them - then snap under pressure. Real strength looks more like a tree: grounded, but able to move with what life brings.

Today, let a tree remind you how you want to stand in your life. Notice its roots (even if you can't see them), its trunk, and its branches. It didn't get here overnight. It grew ring by ring, season by season. You're doing the same. Your habits, your thoughts, and your relationships are your roots. When you deepen them in healthy soil, you don't have to white-knuckle every storm. You know you can sway without breaking.

Today's Nudge:
Spend a few minutes near a tree. Stand with your feet planted, shoulders relaxed, and imagine yourself rooted like it is. Breathe there.

Daily Anchor: "I choose to be rooted and flexible, not rigid and easily broken."

Reflection

- In what areas of your life do you feel rooted?
- Where do you feel like you could be knocked over easily?

17 Change with the Seasons

"You are not meant to be in permanent summer."

Nature doesn't apologize for changing. There's a time for growth, a time for shedding, a time for rest, and a time for starting again. Men get into trouble when they expect themselves to be in "go mode" all year: always productive, always high-energy, and always on. When you refuse to acknowledge your seasons, you burn out or feel like a failure for needing rest or transition. But just like nature, your life has winters, springs, summers, and falls.

Today, instead of fighting your current season, name it. Maybe you're in a "winter," where things feel slow or quiet or unclear. Maybe you're in a "spring," starting something new. Each season asks something different of you. Winter invites rest and reflection. Spring invites courage and small beginnings. Summer invites full effort. Fall invites release. When you understand the season you're in, you can pace yourself with more honesty and less shame.

Today's Nudge:
Look around outside and notice signs of the current season where you live. Then, honestly name what season your life is in right now.

Daily Anchor: "I respect the season I'm in and adjust my pace accordingly."

Reflection

- How have you been fighting your current season?
- What might change if you worked with it instead of against it?

18 Flow Like Water

"Not everything needs to be forced."

Water is powerful, but it's rarely in a hurry. It flows around rocks, finds cracks, and takes the path that's available instead of getting stuck trying to punch through everything in its way. Many men only know how to push. When something doesn't move, they either slam harder or shut down. There's a third option: flowing, which doesn't mean giving up; it means adjusting your route while keeping your direction.

Today, let water remind you that you don't have to fight every obstacle head-on. Some things you push through. Others you move around. Your insistence on forcing some relationships, habits, and goals might be exhausting you. Flow asks: is there a different angle, a smaller step, or a more natural route? Learning when to push and when to flow is a skill that protects your energy and keeps you moving.

Today's Nudge:
Spend a few moments near water if you can: a river, a fountain, or even a shower. Think of one situation where you've been forcing things and ask, "What would flowing look like in this situation?"

Daily Anchor: "I know when to push and when to flow."

Reflection

- Where in your life are you pushing so hard that you're wearing yourself out?
- What might happen if you tried a more flexible approach?

19 Weather the Storm

"Feelings are weather, not destiny."

Storms roll in, do their damage, and eventually move on. They can be intense, loud, and messy, but they are temporary. Your emotions, whether anger, sadness, anxiety, or frustration, work the same way. When a storm hits your life, it's easy to believe "this is who I am now" or "it's always going to be like this." That belief traps you. Seeing emotions as weather lets you experience them without letting them define you.

Today, if your mood feels stormy, try labeling it as weather: "This rough front is passing through," instead of "I'm broken." You still take cover and respond wisely, but you stop confusing the storm with the whole sky. Even on cloudy days, the sky is behind the clouds. In the same way, there's more to you than whatever you're feeling in this moment.

Today's Nudge:
When you feel a strong emotion today, pause and name it as "weather" instead of judgment (e.g., "I'm in a storm of frustration right now"). Notice how that shifts your response.

Daily Anchor: "My emotions are weather; they move through me, but they are not all of me."

Reflection

- What emotional "storm" has been hanging over you lately?
- How does it feel to see it as passing weather instead of your permanent state?

20 Look at the Horizon

"When you lift your eyes, your problems shrink back into perspective."

When you're stuck in stress, your vision narrows. You only see the urgent email, the bill, the conflict, or the next task. It feels like your entire life is this one problem or one season. Nature has a simple antidote for tunnel vision: the horizon. When you look at a wide view, whether across water, over rooftops, or across fields, you remember the world is bigger than your current situation. That perspective doesn't erase your problems, but it puts them back in context.

Today, give your eyes and mind some distance. Take a moment to look as far as you can see. Breathe while you do it. Imagine your life stretched out ahead of you: not just this week, but the next few years. The choices you're making now around pace, movement, and nature are not just about surviving today. They're shaping the man you'll be later. When you remember that, it's easier to be patient with slow progress and less dramatic about temporary setbacks.

Today's Nudge:
Find a spot where you can see a wide view: a hill, rooftop, open field, long street, or balcony. Spend a few minutes just looking out and breathing.

Daily Anchor: "I lift my eyes and remember my life is bigger than this moment."

Reflection

- How does your current stress look when you imagine your life 1-5 years from now?
- What kind of man do you want to be standing on that future horizon?

21 Week Three Debrief

"Nature is a mirror; what you see outside often reflects what's happening inside."

This week, you chose a spot, watched trees, noticed seasons, observed water, lived through some emotional "weather," and lifted your eyes to the horizon. You weren't just sightseeing; you were letting nature talk back to you. The goal of Week 3 was to help you realize that you're not separate from nature; you're part of it. Your pace, your stress, your growth, and your rest is connected to the environment you put yourself in.

Think back over the last seven days. When did nature help you slow your pace? When did it give you a metaphor or picture that stuck with you, like the tree, the storm, or the horizon? Those images are tools you can carry forward. In future stressful moments, you'll be able to remember, "This is weather," or "I'm in a winter," or "I need to flow, not force." That's how nature becomes a coach that you can access any time.

Today's Nudge:
Review Days 15-20. Write down one nature image or lesson from this week that hit you the hardest and how you want to use it going forward.

Daily Anchor: "I let nature teach me how to pace my life."

Reflection

- Which practice from this week felt most natural to you?
- Which felt most uncomfortable?
- What is that telling you about how you've been living?

22 Who You're Becoming

"Your habits follow your identity, not the other way around."

Most men try to change their lives by changing isolated behaviors; you may eat better, work out, or become more disciplined without touching the deeper question: "Who am I becoming?" If you see yourself as the same old guy who always quits, always procrastinates, or always falls back into the same patterns, your habits will eventually return to match that identity. When you start to see yourself differently, your daily choices have somewhere new to land.

Today, you're going to name the man you're becoming: not in a cheesy way, but in a clear, grounded sentence. Think of the kind of man you want to be in five years: how he treats his body, how he handles stress, how he shows up for people, and how he moves through the world. Then, bring him into the present tense: "I am a man who..." You're not pretending that you're already there. You're setting the direction that your pace will follow.

Today's Nudge:
Write a one-sentence "Who I'm Becoming" statement that starts with "I am a man who..." Read it out loud at least once today.

Daily Anchor: "I pace my life in line with the man I'm becoming."

Reflection

- How have you been unconsciously defining yourself up to now?
- How does your new statement shift the way you see your daily choices?

23 You're Not Meant to Go Alone

"Lone-wolf living feels strong at first and empty in the long run."

A lot of men carry the belief that real strength means handling everything alone. Asking for help, being honest about what's really going on in your life, or sharing your emotions feels like weakness. The problem is isolation quietly eats away at you. You can look fine on the outside and be slowly falling apart inside because no one knows what's going on with you. Having even one man in your life who knows the real story can change everything about your pace and resilience.

You don't need a huge group or a perfect "men's circle" to start. You just need one step toward connection. That step might mean texting a friend you've drifted from, being more honest with someone you already trust, or saying yes to an invite you'd usually dodge. Community doesn't have to be dramatic; it can start with simply deciding, "I won't carry all of this by myself anymore."

Today's Nudge:
Reach out to one man today, whether a friend, coworker, or relative, and check in for real. Ask how he's doing and share one honest sentence about how you're doing.

Daily Anchor: "I am strong enough to not walk this road alone."

Reflection

- Where have you been trying to go alone?
- What fears come up when you think about letting another man see the real you?

24 Be a Safe Place

"The kind of man you are to others shapes the kind of men that want to be around you."

Every man wants people in his life who are solid, trustworthy, and real. But, it starts with becoming that kind of man yourself. Being a "safe place" doesn't mean you fix everyone's problems or always know what to say. It means people feel they can be honest around you without being mocked, minimized, or ignored. It means you listen more than you lecture, and you privately keep what they share with you.

Today, you can practice being the kind of man who makes it easier for others to be honest. That practice might look like going first - being honest when someone asks how you're doing, instead of defaulting to "I'm good," and not hiding behind jokes when something real is going on. When you are a safe place for others, you create the conditions for real connection, and you make it more likely that they'll show up for you when you need it.

Today's Nudge:
In one conversation today, focus on listening fully. Ask one deeper follow-up question and resist the urge to jump straight into advice or jokes.

Daily Anchor: "I am a man others can be real with."

Reflection

- How do people usually feel after talking to you: lighter, heard, dismissed, talked over?
- What would it look like to be a "safe place" in your circles?

25 Show Up When It's Boring

"The boring days build the man you become."

Motivation is loud but unreliable. It shows up when things feel new or exciting and disappears when progress gets slow and repetitive. Most transformation doesn't happen on the big, dramatic days; it happens on the boring ones, when no one is watching, and you're tempted to skip. Showing up on those days is how you prove to yourself that your pace is no longer controlled by feelings alone.

Today is about honoring your baseline even if nothing in you feels like it. Do the walk. Do the breathing. Visit your spot. Read the entry. Not because these things are thrilling, but because of who you are now: a man who keeps small promises to himself. Every time you do what you said you'd do on a low-motivation day, you quietly rebuild trust with yourself. That trust is priceless.

Today's Nudge:
Do your chosen baseline habit today even if you're tired, grumpy, or busy. No upgrades and no extras, just the baseline.

Daily Anchor: "I show up even when it's not exciting."

Reflection

- How have you treated "boring" days in the past?
- What story could you start telling yourself about what it means when you show up anyway?

26 Upgrade Your Default

"Big change is usually just a series of small upgrades."

Most of your life runs on default settings: what you eat without thinking, how late you stay up, what you do when stressed, and where you go when you're bored. You don't need to overhaul everything at once. You just need to upgrade a few key defaults so that the "automatic" choices you make are slightly more aligned with the man you're becoming. Think of it like a software update: same system, better performance.

Today, pick one default you can nudge in a healthier direction. Maybe it's swapping one late-night scroll session for 15 extra minutes of sleep. Maybe it's walking during one break instead of sitting the whole time. Maybe it's drinking water before that second soda or beer. Small upgrades don't look impressive on their own, but over months and years, they quietly change your trajectory.

Today's Nudge:
Choose one default behavior (sleep, food, movement, screen time, environment) and upgrade it by one small, concrete step today.

***Daily Anchor: "I improve my life by upgrading my defaults,
one at a time."***

Reflection

- What default have you been running that clearly doesn't serve you anymore?
- What simple upgrade would make your future self grateful?

27 Your Quiet Legacy

"Who you are in the small moments is what people actually remember."

When men think about "legacy," they often picture big achievements, such as titles, money, or awards. Those things can matter, but most people will remember you for how you lived day-to-day: how you treated them, whether they felt safe around you, or whether your presence brought calm or chaos. Your quiet legacy is being written right now in small habits, tiny interactions, and subtle choices.

Today, imagine someone close to you describing you years from now. What words do you want them to use? Steady. Present. Honest. Kind. Strong. Those qualities aren't built by grand gestures. They're built by small, repeated actions, such as showing up, apologizing when you mess up, taking care of your health, and keeping your word. Every time you choose a slightly healthier pace, you're shaping that legacy.

Today's Nudge:
Do one small action today that future people in your life (or your future self) would be proud to mention when they talk about you.

Daily Anchor: "My daily choices are shaping a quiet legacy I can be proud of."

Reflection

- If someone had to describe your current daily legacy in three words, what might they be?
- What three words do you want to move toward?

28 Future You Needs You Now

"The man you want to be is built today, not someday."

It's easy to imagine a "future you" who magically has it all together; he is fit, calm, confident, disciplined, and grounded. But, that man doesn't appear out of nowhere. He's the result of hundreds of small decisions you make when no one is watching. Every time you choose your baseline, step outside, breathe, or rest on purpose, you're casting a vote for that future version of you. Every time you ignore your needs and numb out, you're voting for a different outcome.

Today, you don't need to become future you overnight. You just need to do one thing he would thank you for. Think of him, not as some stranger, but as you with more miles, more responsibilities, and more people depending on him. What kind of condition do you want to hand his life back to him in? When you move, rest, connect, and reflect today, you're putting something in his account.

Today's Nudge:
Write down three things future you (5-10 years from now) will have because of the habits you're starting or strengthening now. Do one small action today that serves him.

*Daily Anchor: "I will live today in a way that takes care of
my future self."*

Reflection

- When you picture future you honestly, what do you hope is different about his life and pace?
- What decisions today move you closer to that picture?

29 Keep the Pace

"Consistency beats intensity, especially after the "program" ends."

You're near the end of these 30 days. A common trap is to go hard for a month, feel good about the streak, and then slide back into old patterns once the structure is gone. The goal of "Pace Your Self" was never to give you a perfect month; it was to help you find a way of living that you can sustain. Keeping the pace means choosing a small set of practices you carry forward instead of trying to hold on to everything.

Today, you'll narrow down. Look back across the whole month and ask, What 2-3 practices made the biggest difference for my mood, energy, or sense of control? That practice might be your daily walk, your breathing break, your time at your outdoor spot, your nightly gauge check, or your identity statement. Those practices become your core. If you keep them, your pace will stay different, even without this book in your hands.

Today's Nudge:
Choose 2-3 practices from this month that you commit to keeping as your core "pace" habits going forward. Write them down somewhere you'll see daily.

Daily Anchor: "I choose a realistic pace I can sustain beyond these 30 days."

Reflection

- What have you learned about what works for you, not just what sounds good?
- How can you protect these few practices in your schedule?

30 Pace Your Self

"Your life is not a sprint; it's a long, personal race with your name on it."

You've spent 30 days paying attention to your mind, your body, and your environment. You've walked, breathed, noticed, rested, and reflected. Some days probably felt powerful; others may have felt like a miss or a mess. That's real life. The most important thing is you now know more about your pace than you did a month ago. You've seen how small shifts in movement, nature, and attention affect how you feel and who you're becoming.

Today is not an ending; it's a marker. You're stepping into the next stretch of your race with better information and more tools. "Pace Your Self" means you don't have to match anyone else's speed, story, or path. You can move slower and deeper than the world says you "should" and still become the strongest version of yourself. Your job now is to keep listening to your body, your environment, and your values and keep adjusting your pace so that you can go the distance.

Today's Nudge:
Write a short, personal "Pace Your Self" declaration: a few sentences about how you intend to move through life, physically, mentally, and emotionally, from here.

Daily Anchor: "This is my race, my pace, and I choose to walk it as the man I'm becoming."

Reflection

- What has changed in you over these 30 days, even if it's subtle?
- What commitments about your pace do you want to carry into the next season of your life?

After the 30 Days: Keep Pacing Your Self

Today is not the finish line. It's just the first mile.

You've made it through 30 days of paying attention to your pace. You've learned to slow down, move intentionally, listen to nature, and rethink what kind of man you're becoming. But, here's the truth few books tell you: lasting change is about learning to live in your personal pace every day for the long haul, not a one-time sprint or perfect month.

Remember the habits and practices that truly stuck for you: the 2 or 3 core things you committed to keeping after this book is done because they are your anchors. Your "Who I'm Becoming" statement is your compass. When life speeds up or throws storms, it's easy to lose your way. You might skip walks, scroll more, or forget to check in with yourself. That's normal. When it happens, don't give up or get down on yourself. Return to your baseline. Return to your pace.

Your journey shouldn't end here. It should expand. This book is a map, and you are the explorer. You have the tools to keep pacing yourself through whatever life brings, whether changing jobs, starting relationships, facing challenges, or finding peace. Whenever you feel lost, revisit your favorite chapters, reconnect with your outdoor spot, check your gauges, and remind yourself that this is your race, your pace, and your story.

Consider sharing this journey with another man. Accountability isn't just a tool; it's a catalyst for growth. Who you become is shaped not only by your steps, but also by the footsteps you walk alongside.

Today, take a moment to breathe in how far you've come and look ahead with quiet confidence. The greatest victory is not rushing to the finish but having the strength to keep showing up, day after day, pacing yourself as the man you're becoming.

Daily Anchor: "I will keep pacing myself, steady and strong, through every inch, every foot, and every mile of my life."

Conclusion

You have arrived at the end of these 30 days, but not the end of your journey. Pace Your Self began as an invitation to listen deeply to your body, mind, and spirit so that you could find a rhythm that honors your uniqueness.

Remember, pacing is a lifelong practice rather than a one-time event or quick fix. The tools, reflections, and nudges you have engaged with are seeds for a way of living marked by patience, presence, and purpose.

As you move forward, carry with you the truth that strength is built in steady steps, that progress is measured against your growth, and that every day offers a new chance to pace yourself well.

Return to this book whenever you need to recalibrate and consider sharing this journey with other men. Together, we find balance, power, and peace.

Your race is your own. Keep pacing yourself with grace and courage.

Appendix: The Science Behind Pacing, Movement, and Nature

The tools and philosophies in *Pace Your Self* are grounded in decades of peer-reviewed research across various disciplines, including environmental psychology, neuroscience, and mental health. This body of evidence confirms that consistent movement and intentional exposure to restorative environments, especially nature, are not optional lifestyle enhancements, but biological necessities for a well-regulated nervous system and sustainable well-being.[1]

1. Stress Reduction and Physiological Restoration

Human beings evolved in close relationship with natural environments, and our nervous systems remain wired to respond to them. Stress Reduction Theory explains why exposure to nature produces an immediate, involuntary calming effect, particularly after stress or exertion.[2]

Research demonstrates that contact with natural settings positively influences core physiological markers of stress, including heart rate, blood pressure, and cortisol levels.[3] After stressful experiences, time spent in non-threatening natural environments accelerates recovery and reduces overall arousal.[4]

Field experiments further show that spending time in urban parks and forested environments significantly increases feelings of restoration and subjective vitality when compared to remaining in dense city centers.[5] Blue spaces, environments that include water, have also been associated with enhanced relaxation, social connection, and improved overall well-being.[6]

2. Attention Restoration and Mental Clarity

When men describe feeling mentally "fried," overwhelmed, or unable to focus, they are often experiencing Directed Attention Fatigue (DAF) which is a depletion of the cognitive resources required for sustained concentration. Attention Restoration Theory explains how nature serves as a restorative counterbalance.[7]

Natural environments engage the mind through what researchers call *soft fascination*: stimuli such as rustling leaves, moving water, or shifting light that gently hold attention without effort. This allows the brain's executive systems to rest and replenish.[8]

Studies show that interacting with nature, through walking, sitting outdoors, or even viewing images of natural scenes, improves performance on tasks requiring attention, working memory, and cognitive flexibility.[9] Notably, these benefits are not limited to wilderness immersion; even brief exposure can yield measurable improvements.[10]

3. Emotional Regulation and Nervous System Balance

Regular exposure to natural environments has been consistently linked to improved mood, reduced rumination, and enhanced emotional regulation.[11] Nature-based mindfulness practices support greater self-awareness and emotional clarity, strengthening key components of emotional intelligence.[12]

Clinical and therapeutic research in ecotherapy and related approaches indicates that engaging with nature can support individuals experiencing anxiety, depression, chronic stress, and burnout by helping the nervous system downshift from survival mode into regulation.[13]

4. The Power of Brief Exposure and Environmental Anchors

The benefits of nature do not require extended retreats or dramatic lifestyle changes. One of the most influential findings in this field, often referred to as *the window effect*, revealed that hospital patients with views of nature recovered faster and required less pain medication than those whose windows faced brick walls.[14]

Subsequent research has shown that even short periods, approximately 10 to 20 minutes, of exposure to natural elements can promote attentional recovery and emotional reset.[15] Incorporating indoor plants, window views, or brief outdoor pauses into daily routines has been associated with reduced physiological and psychological stress and healthier brainwave patterns.[16]

This is why *Pace Your Self* emphasizes strategic rest and environmental anchors. Pacing is not about stopping; it is about choosing recovery environments that support resilience rather than drain it.

5. Broad Relevance Across Men's Lives and Lifestyles

Nature- and movement-based approaches to mental health have demonstrated effectiveness across diverse populations, professions, and life stages. Research indicates that men who perceive greater benefits from nature, feel more connected to natural environments, or had meaningful exposure earlier in life are more open to engaging in non-traditional forms of stress support and personal growth.[17]

Clinical observations from my private practice reinforce these findings. Men from a wide range of backgrounds, including athletes, entrepreneurs, creatives, and professionals, often experience meaningful shifts in stress regulation, clarity, and emotional awareness when movement and nature are integrated into their routines.

Think of your nervous system like a smartphone battery. Constant work demands, screen time, and pressure function like high-drain apps that run continuously in the background. Nature exposure acts as a fast-charging station: a brief pause near a window or a short walk offers a quick boost, while deeper immersion provides the full recharge required for long-term endurance.

Notes: Some of the following reference titles have been shortened for brevity.

1. Hartig, T., Mitchell, R., De Vries, S., & Frumkin, H. (2014). Nature and Health. *Annual Review of Public Health, 35*(1), 207-228. https://doi.org/10.1146/annurev-publhealth-032013-182443
2. Ulrich, R. S., Simons, R. F., Losito, B. D., Fiorito, E., Miles, M. A., & Zelson, M. (1991). Stress recovery during exposure to natural and urban environments. *Journal of Environmental Psychology, 11*(3), 201-230. https://doi.org/10.1016/S0272-4944(05)80184-7
3. Ibid.

4. Ulrich, R. S. (1984). View Through a Window May Influence Recovery from Surgery. *Science, 224*(4647), 420–421. https://doi.org/10.1126/science.6143402

5. Tyrväinen, L., Ojala, A., Korpela, K., Lanki, T., Tsunetsugu, Y., & Kagawa, T. (2014). The influence of urban green environments on stress relief measures: A field experiment. *Journal of Environmental Psychology, 38*, 1–9. https://doi.org/10.1016/j.jenvp.2013.12.005

6. White, M. P., Elliott, L. R., Gascon, M., Roberts, B., & Fleming, L. E. (2020). Blue space, health and well-being: A narrative overview and synthesis of potential benefits. *Environmental Research, 191*, 110169. https://doi.org/10.1016/j.envres.2020.110169

7. Kaplan, S. (1995). The restorative benefits of nature: Toward an integrative framework. *Journal of Environmental Psychology, 15*(3), 169–182. https://doi.org/10.1016/0272-4944(95)90001-2

8. Ibid.

9. Berman, M. G., Jonides, J., & Kaplan, S. (2008). The Cognitive Benefits of Interacting With Nature. *Psychological Science, 19*(12), 1207–1212. https://doi.org/10.1111/j.1467-9280.2008.02225.x

10. Ibid.

11. Hartig et al., 2014.

12. Bratman, G. N., Hamilton, J. P., Hahn, K. S., Daily, G. C., & Gross, J. J. (2015). Nature experience reduces rumination and subgenual prefrontal cortex activation. *Proceedings of the National Academy of Sciences, 112*(28), 8567–8572. https://doi.org/10.1073/pnas.1510459112

13. Buzzell, L., & Chalquist, C. (2009). *Ecotherapy*. Sierra Club Books.

14. Ulrich, 1984.

15. Kaplan, 1995.

16. Lee, K. E., Williams, K. J. H., Sargent, L. D., Williams, N. S. G., & Johnson, K. A. (2015). 40-second green roof views sustain attention: The role of micro-breaks in attention restoration. *Journal of Environmental Psychology, 42*, 182–189. https://doi.org/10.1016/j.jenvp.2015.04.003

17. Parker, J. A. (2025). *Exploring Willingness to Participate in Nature-Based Interventions Among Underrepresented Adults*. Dissertation, University of Florida.

About the Author

Dr. Jon A. Parker is a Licensed Professional Counselor in Georgia and a Licensed Mental Health Counselor and Qualified Supervisor in Florida. He helps men reclaim balance, purpose, and a stronger connection to life. In his work, he guides men navigating identity, pressure, relationships, and the quiet expectations many carry alone.

Born in East St. Louis, Illinois, and raised in Southern California, Dr. Parker's path began among boys and young men full of potential—some who found direction and others who lost their way. Seeing both struggle and success planted a lifelong interest in what helps men stay grounded and fulfilled.

After discovering the power of therapy while working at a residential treatment facility in Oakland, California, he pursued graduate studies in Marriage and Family Therapy, later earning a Ph.D. in Youth Development and Family Sciences. His research explores how time in nature restores mental well-being and builds resilience.

A husband, father of four, and lifelong outdoorsman, Dr. Parker founded the Baleka Wellness Initiative and Baleka Run Club in South Africa, where the mantra "Pace Your Self" was born. His work, research, and writing invite men to slow down, reconnect with nature, and live with authenticity—one intentional step at a time.

www.drjparker.me | www.balekawellness.com